Scroll Saw Box
Patterns for boxes

Jeff Vollmer
Jeff D. Vollmer

INTRODUCTION

Building boxes is one of the most rewarding activities when doing woodworking projects. Requiring little material and offering lots of challenges, making a wooden box results in a satisfyingly functional project that is proudly used and displayed or given as a gift that will be cherished for years. It's no wonder boxes rank as the most popular woodworking project by beginners and advanced craftsman alike. This book contains 50 Scroll saw Box Patterns, that bandsaw box enthusiast can use to make beautiful Scroll Saw Boxes. The patterns are one of a kind designs that everyone will love.

Using patterns

Box with scroll saw

This is a box that has a drawer inside to store small objects, it has a unique and attractive shape. To make the box you can use the wood that you like, you can also intersperse different types of wood for its construction.

Materials

- Seven photocopies of the chosen pattern.

- Sheet of reverse teeth number 9 and 5 to cut box profiles and material 2 cm thick.

- 1/16 bit to make the cutting start holes.

- Transparent packaging tape or adhesive tape.

- Sandpaper, grain 80, 150 and 220.

- Drum sander or sandpaper wrapped around a wooden spike.

- Glue for wood.

- Clamps and wooden blocks.

- Rag to clean excess glue.

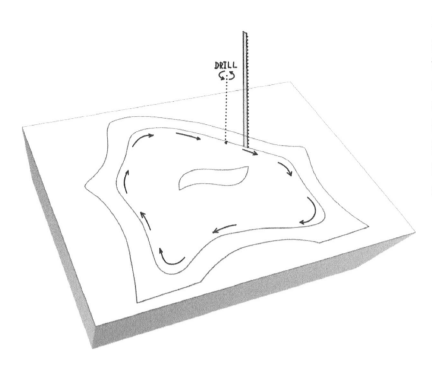

1. Attach a box pattern to each of the seven pieces of material 2 cm thick. Cut five pieces, following the solid lines of the pattern. Do not cut the dashed lines yet.

2. Cut the outer profile into the five pieces and cut a solid piece that I leave uncut, for the back of the drawer.

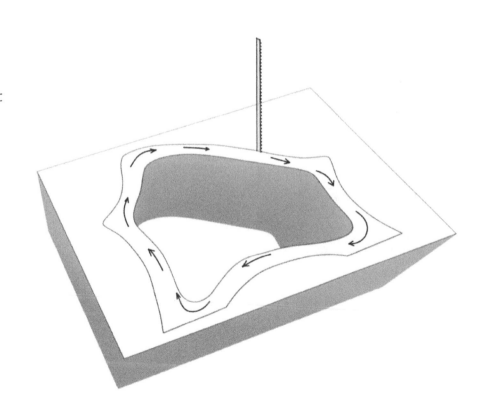

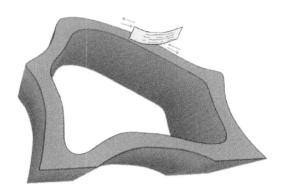

3. Remove the patterns from each of the five pieces of the box. Use alcohol to remove residue from the pattern and remove wood lint with 150 grain sandpaper. Do not remove the pattern from the parts for the inner box.

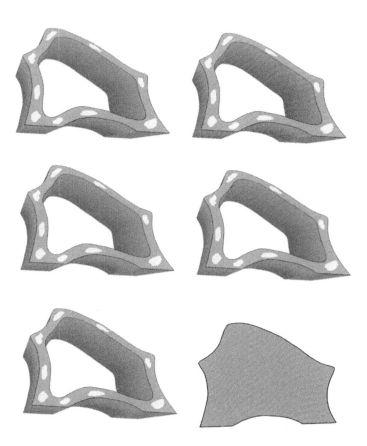

4. Make sure the holes in the parts are aligned. Apply a thin layer of glue to both surfaces of the five box pieces. Do not apply glue to the back of the box.

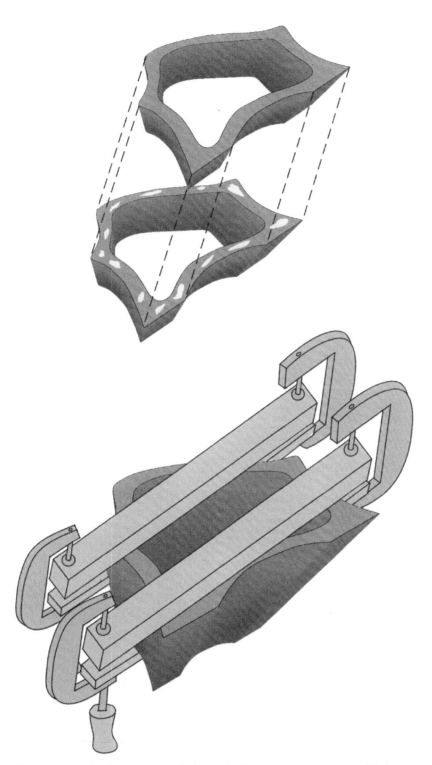

5. Place the five stacked pieces and align all drawer openings. Hold the pieces together using the clamps. Use a cloth to clean the excess glue that appears on the joints. Leave the pieces held for an hour and then release them.

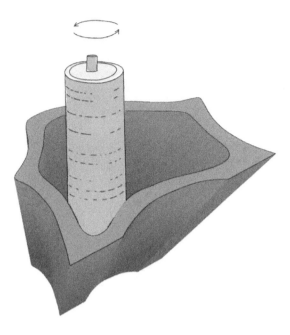

6. Use a drum sander or sandpaper wrapped around a wooden spike to sand the centerpiece of the case until the edges are soft.

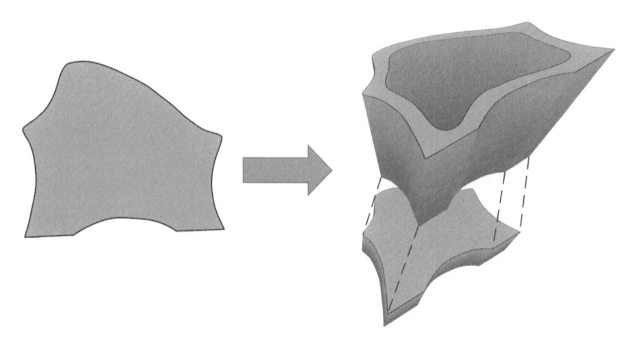

7. Put a thin layer of glue on the surface to be glued on the centerpiece and on the solid back piece of the box. Next, attach the two pieces by aligning the drawer openings. Wait about five minutes for the glue to settle before holding. Clamp the two pieces of the box and let the glue dry.

Inner drawer

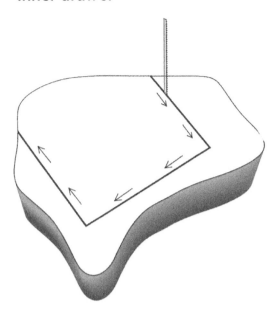

8. Cut three U-shaped pieces and keep two solid pieces for the front and back of the drawer, use a reverse tooth sheet from number 9 to cut the inner drawer compartment by cutting along the dotted lines.

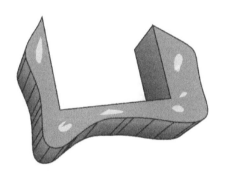

9. Remove patterns from all pieces of drawers and use a sheet of sandpaper to sand the wood lint. For the inner drawer, apply a thin layer of glue to the five pieces. Align the holes and the back and front parts of the drawer.

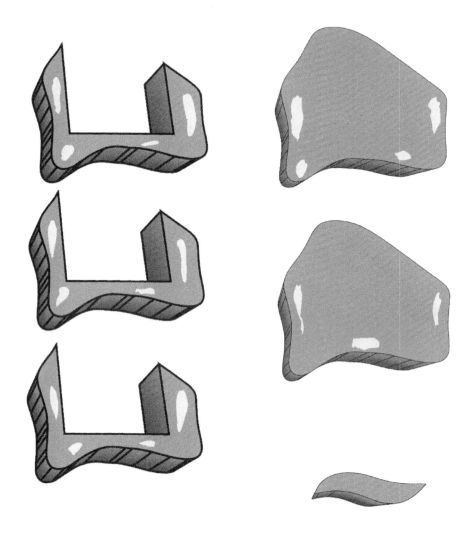

10. Using waste wood blocks, clamp the inner drawer. Remove the glue that slipped out, and then let the glue dry. Then trim the handle using the seventh copy. Stick the drawer handle in the center of the inner drawer.

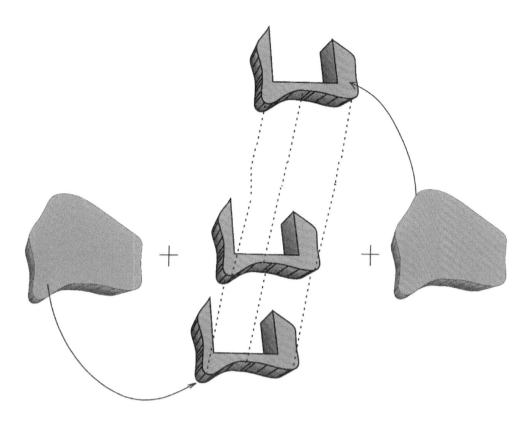

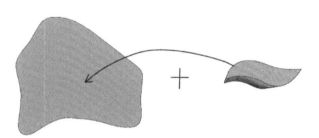

11. Use a drum sander or sandpaper wrapped around a wooden spike to sand both pieces of the case until soft. Apply the finish of your choice and cover the interior compartments with felt or velvet.

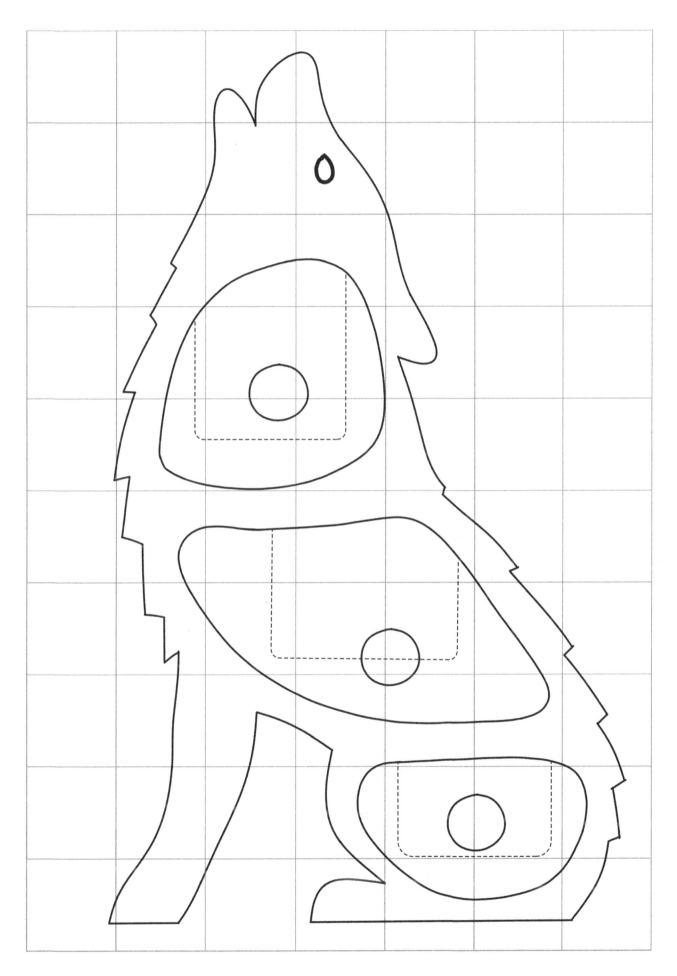

1

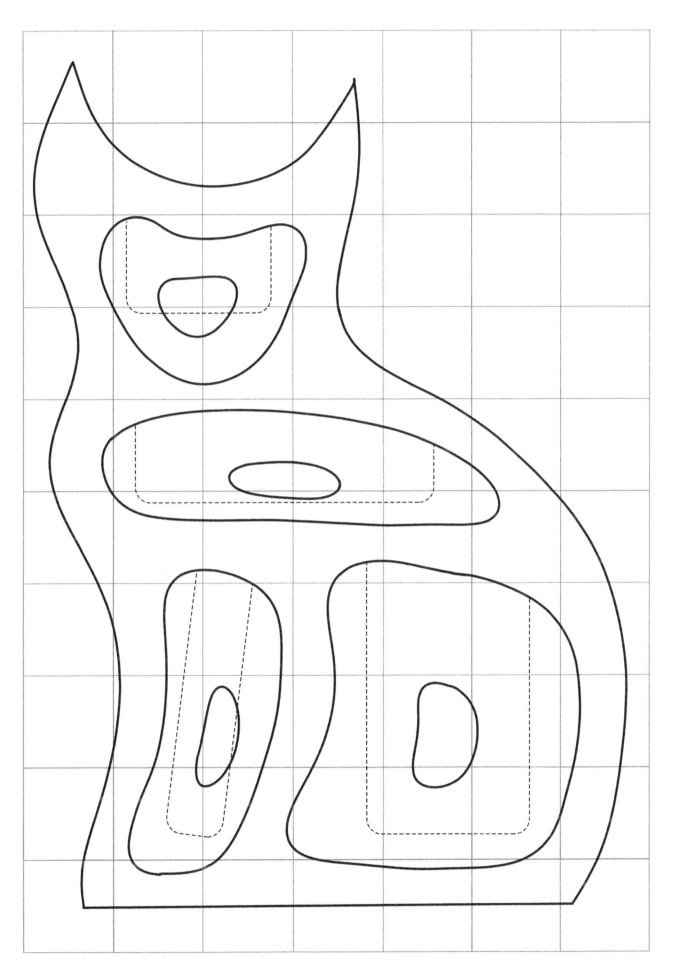

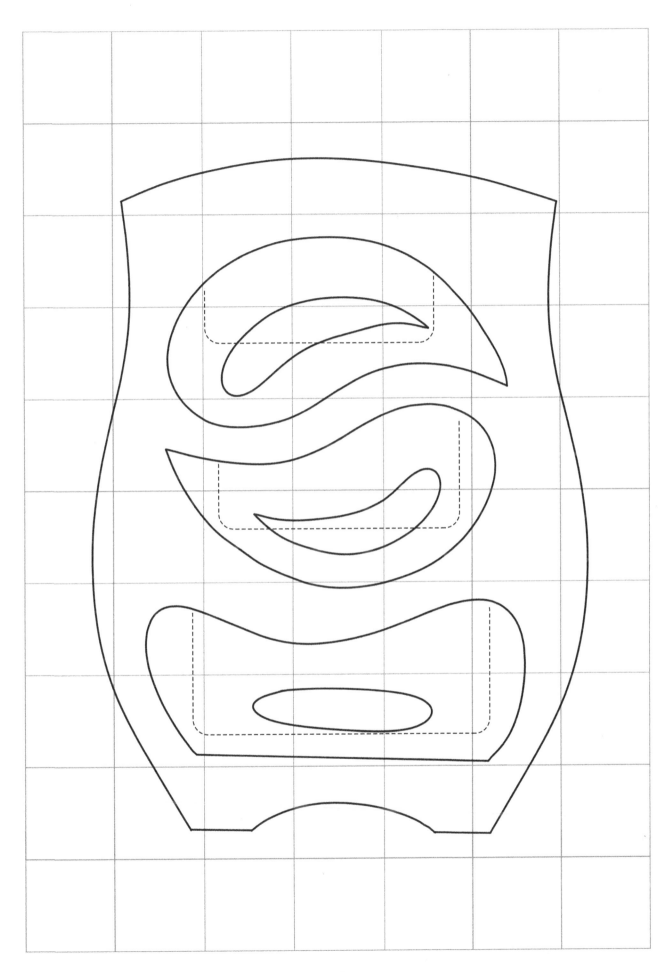

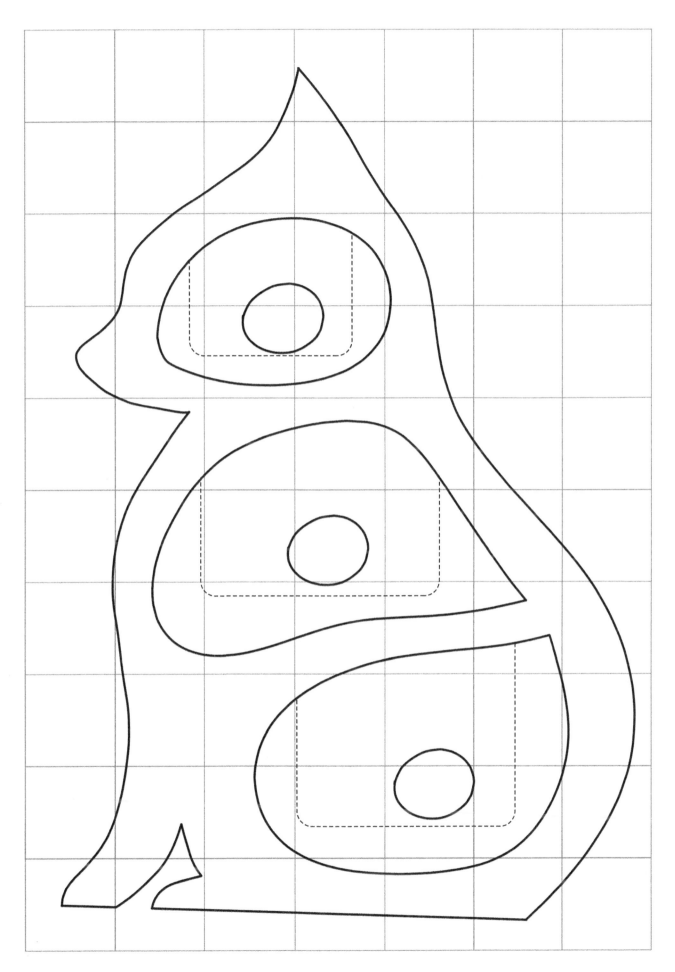

4

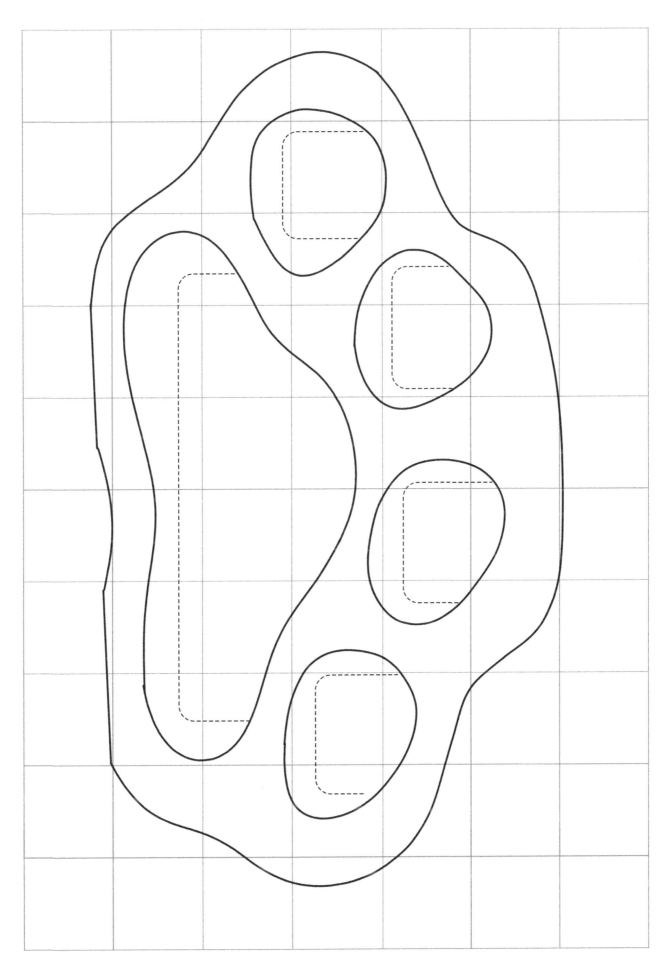

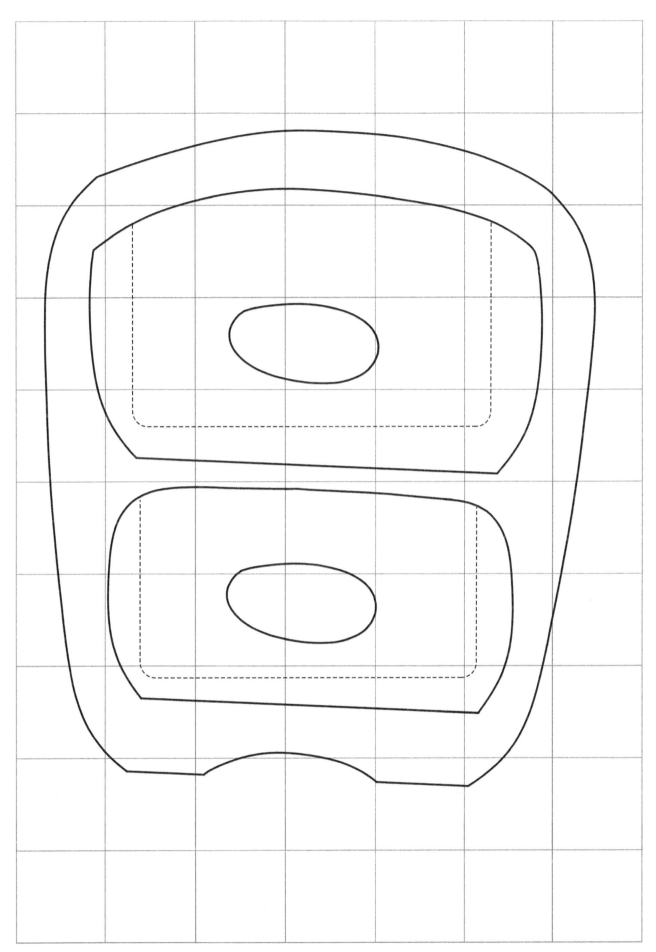

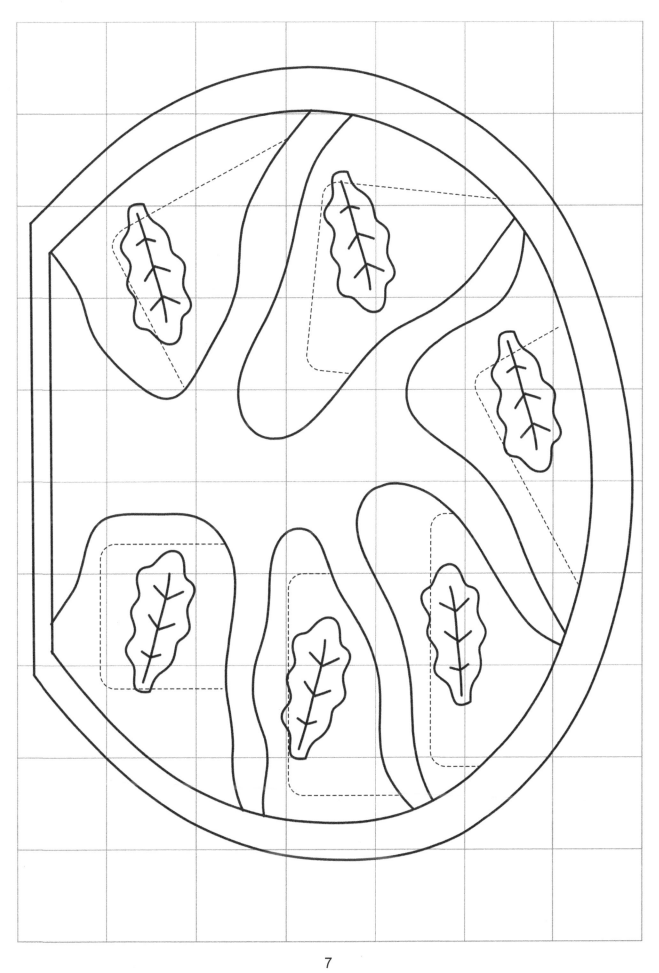

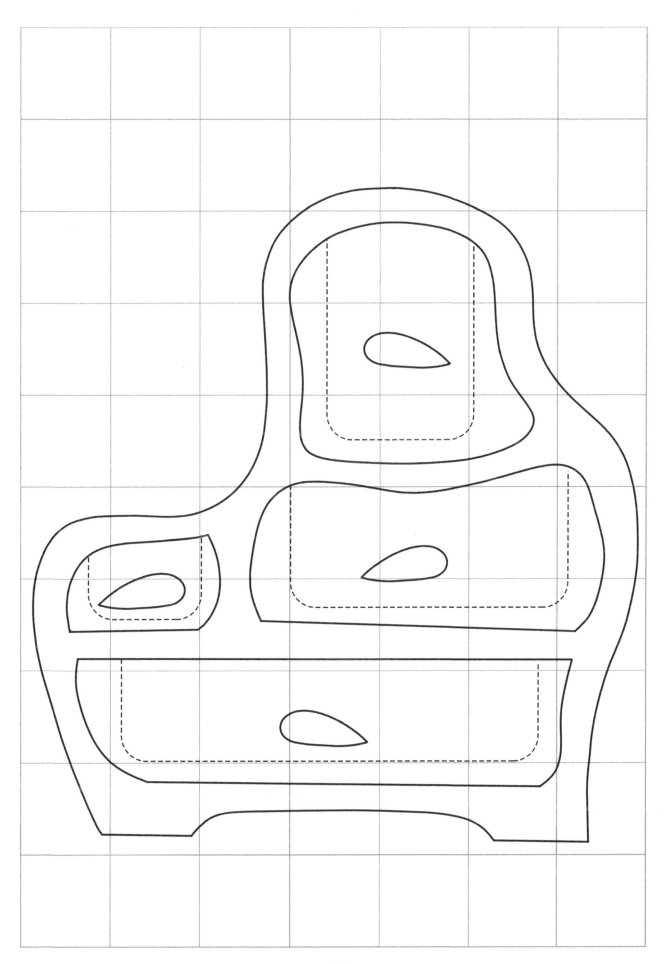

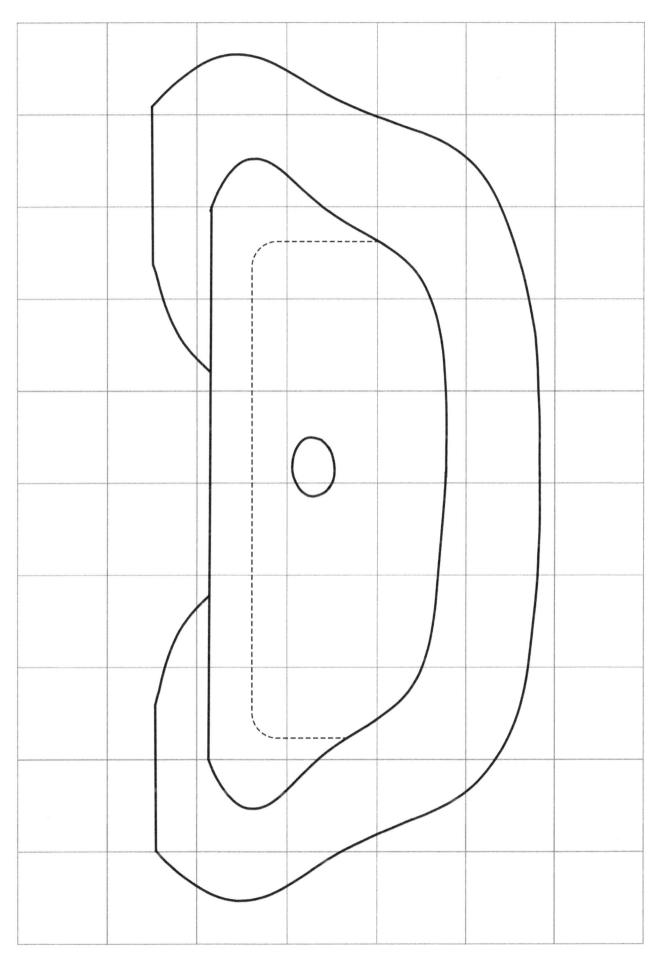

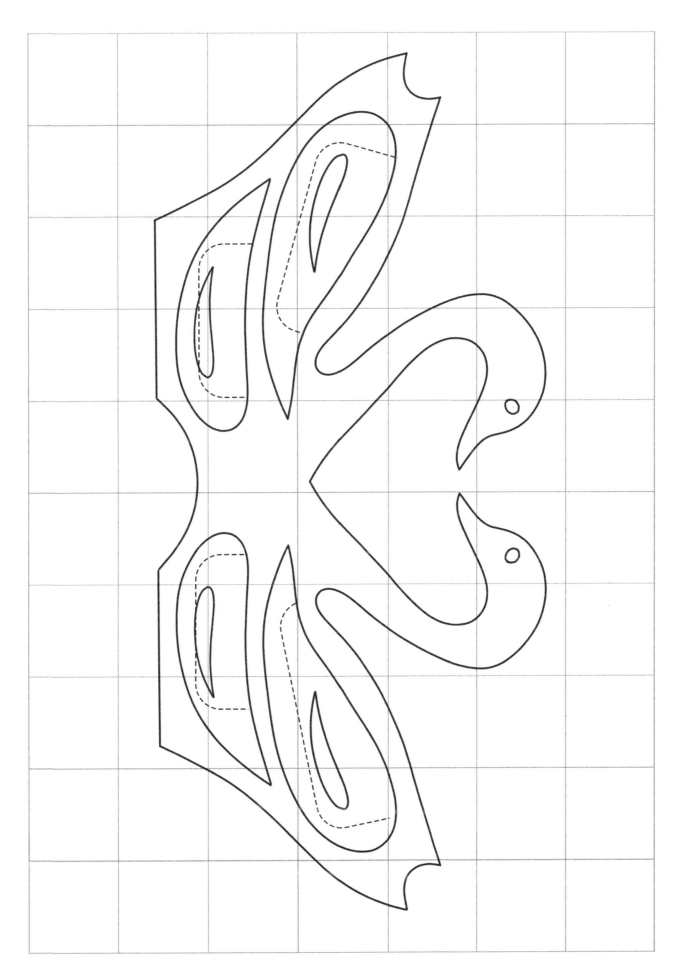

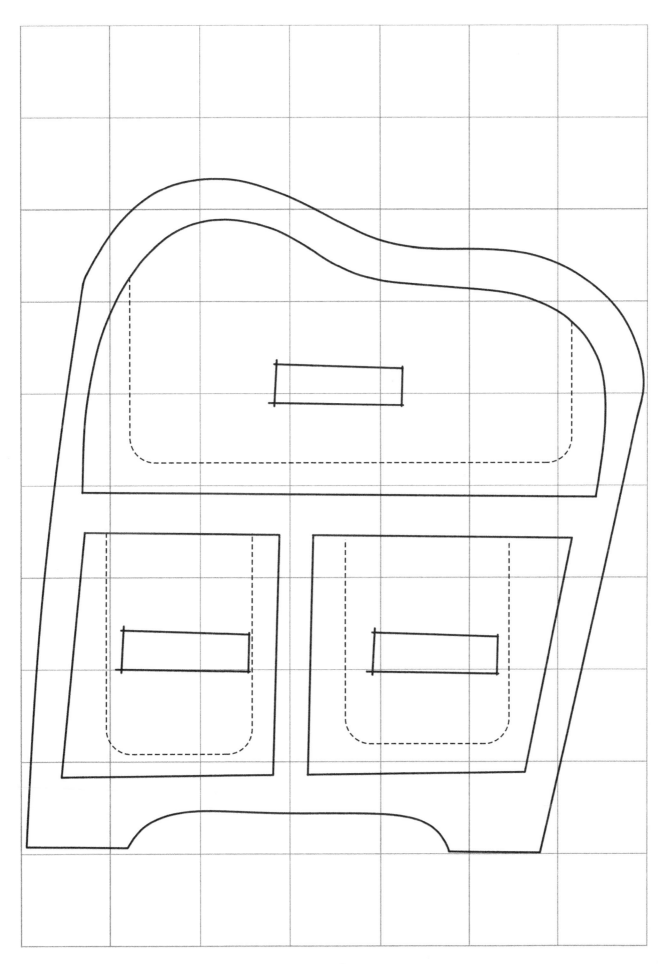

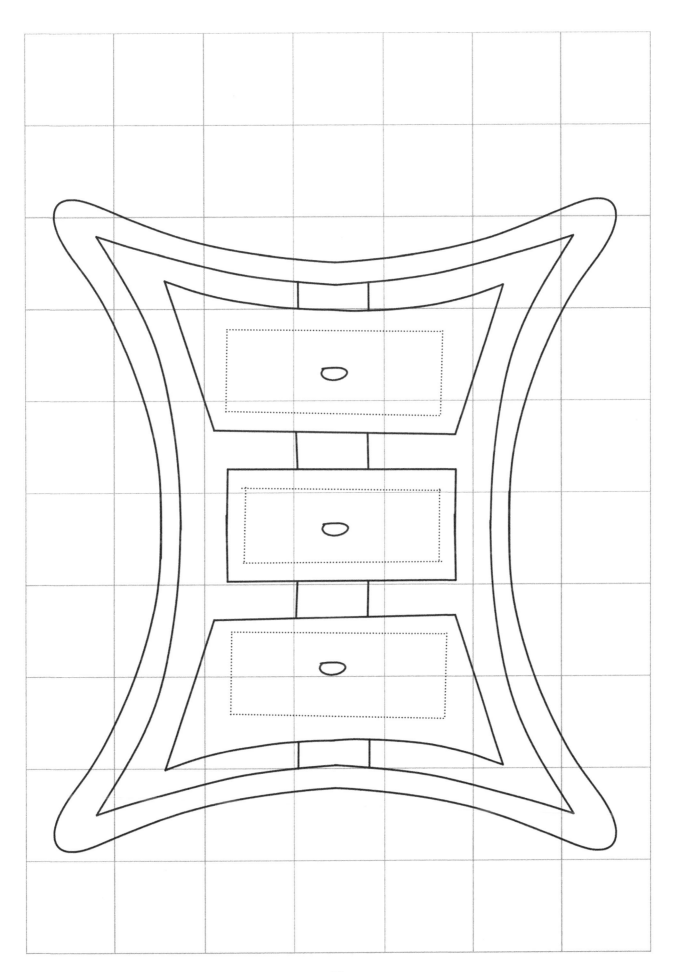

13

14

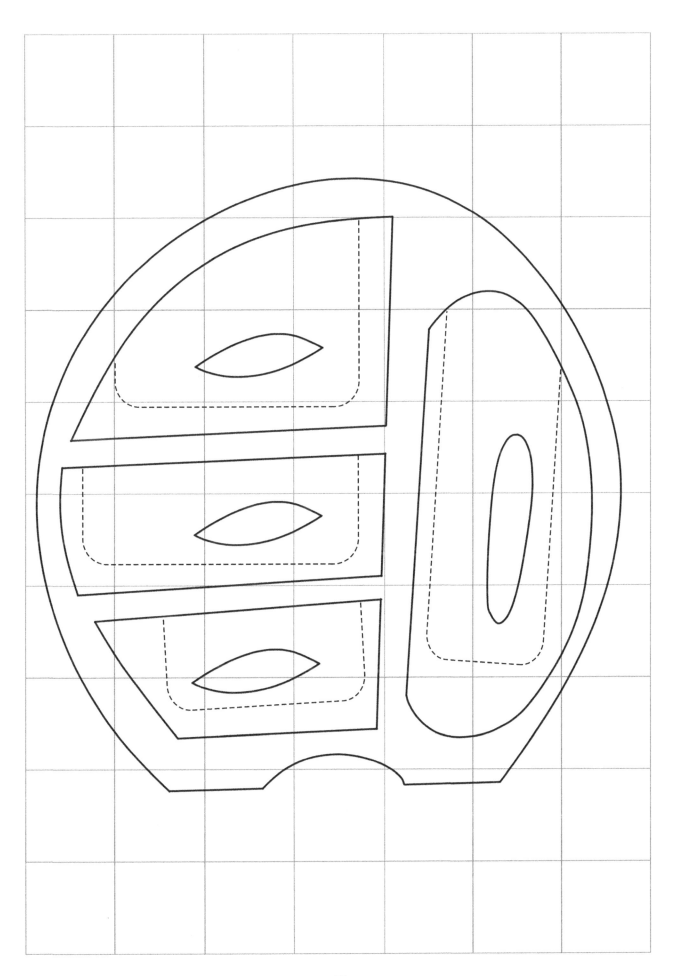

15

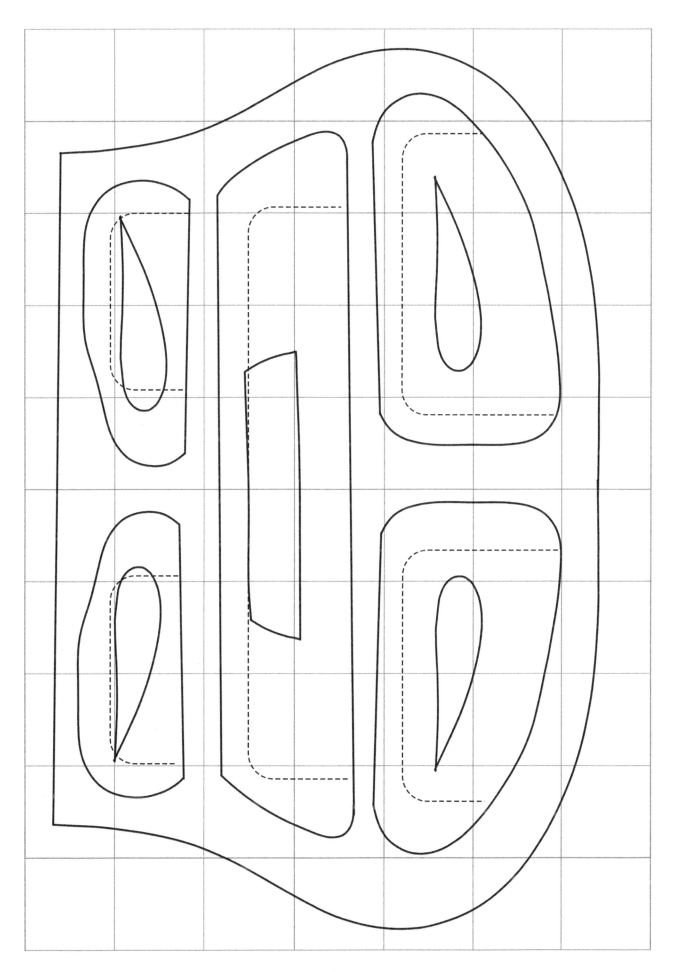

16

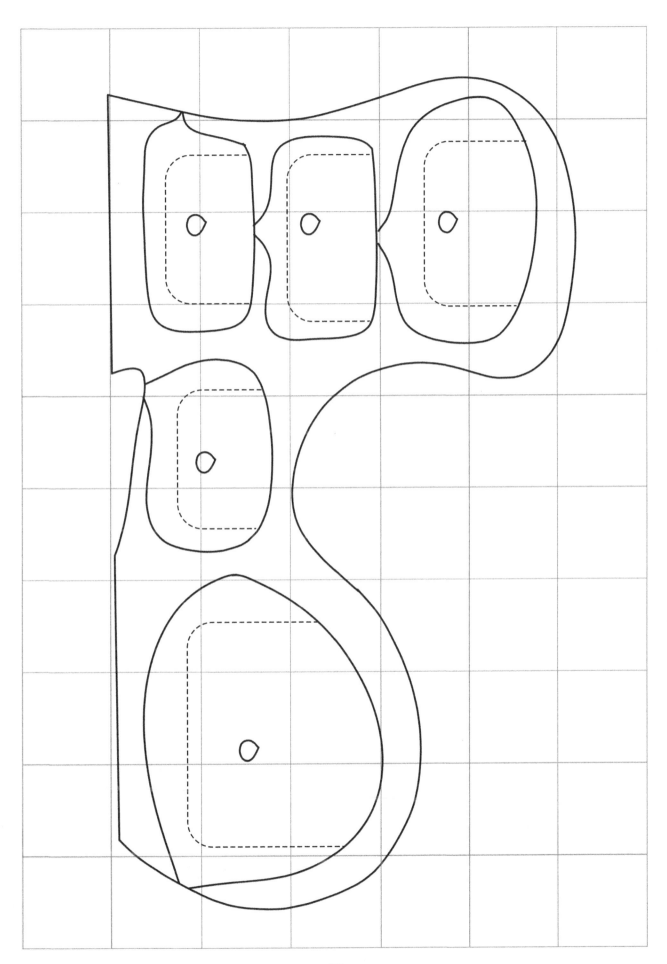

17

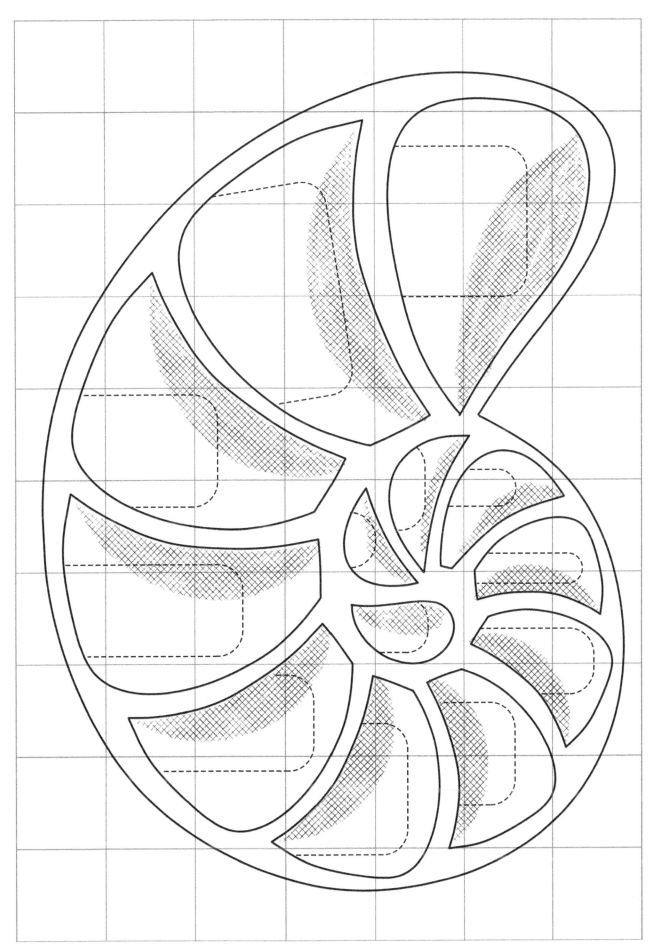

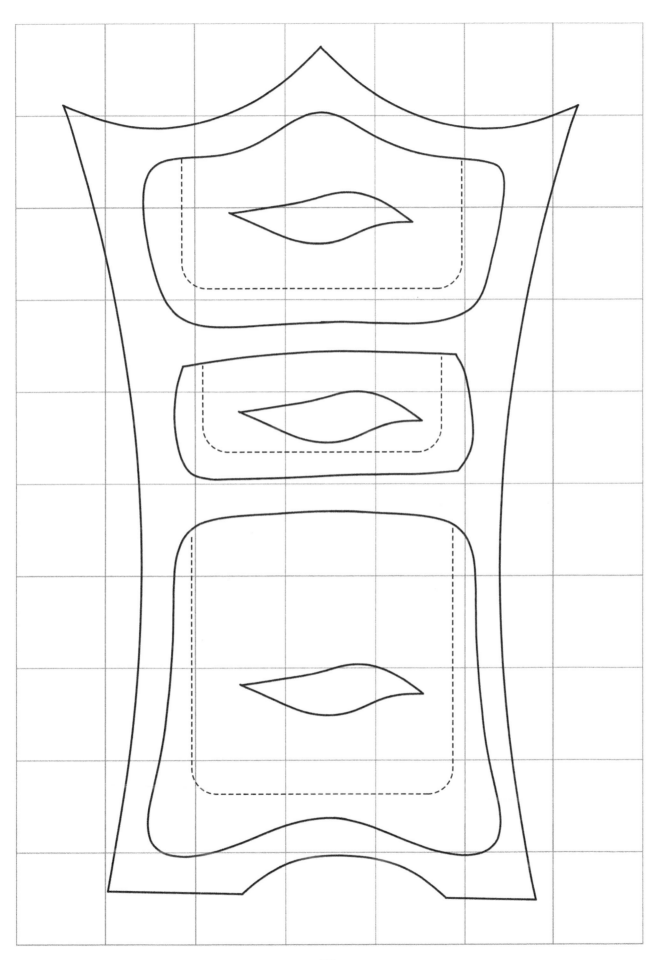

20

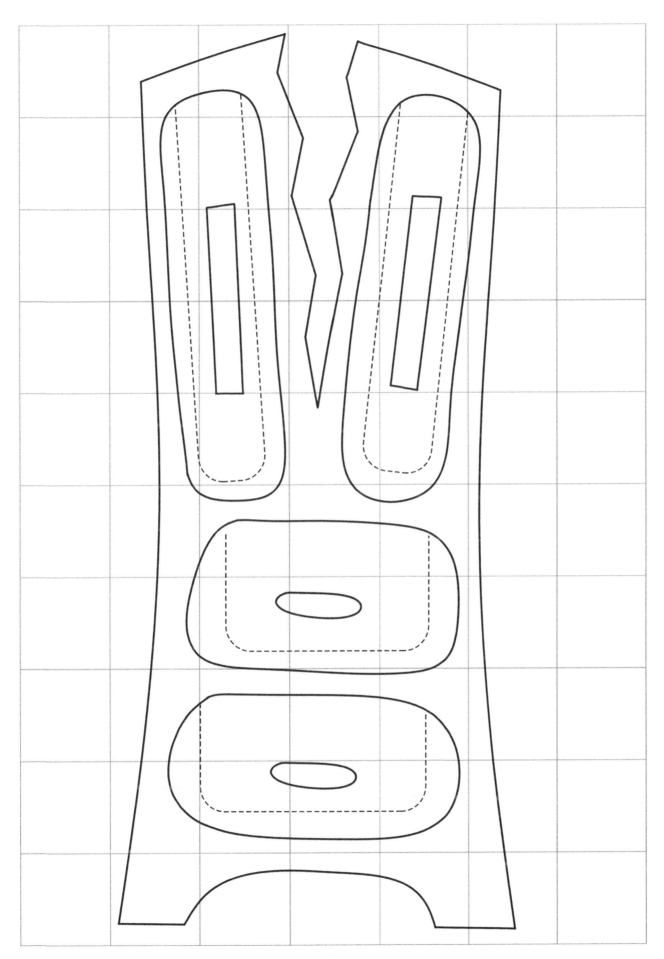

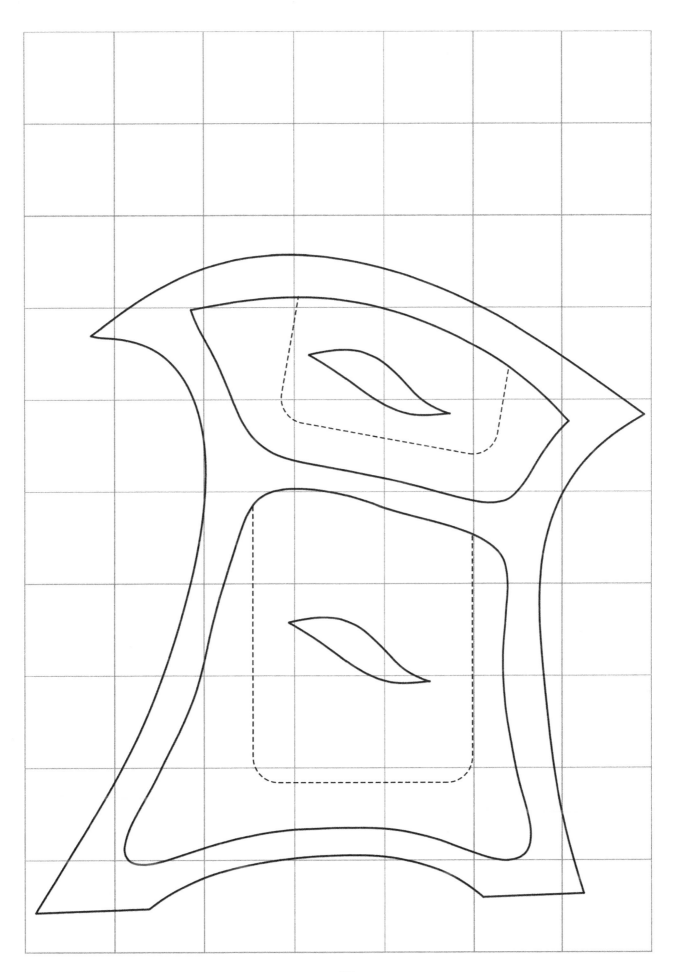

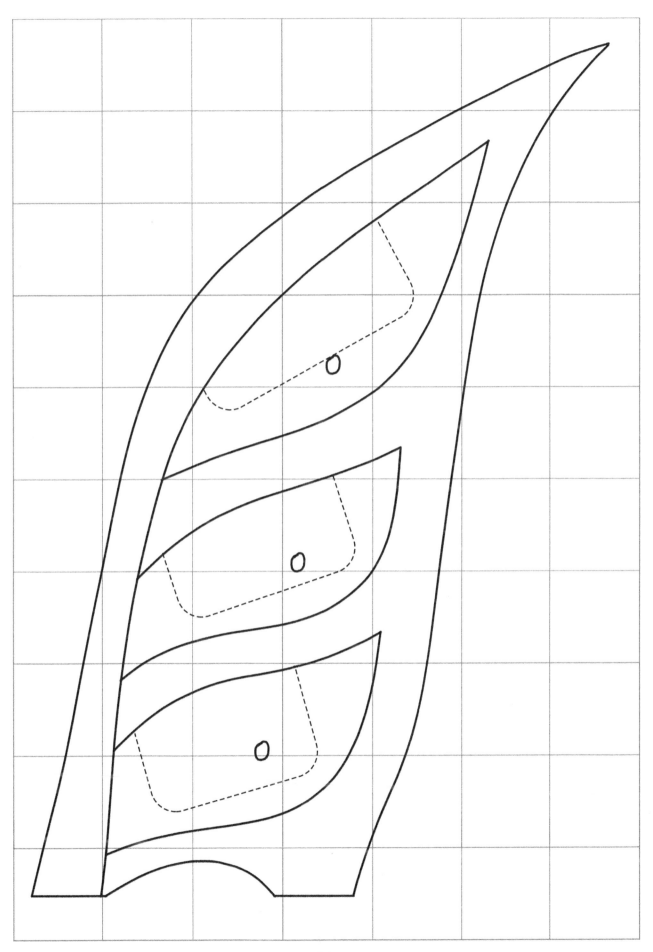

24

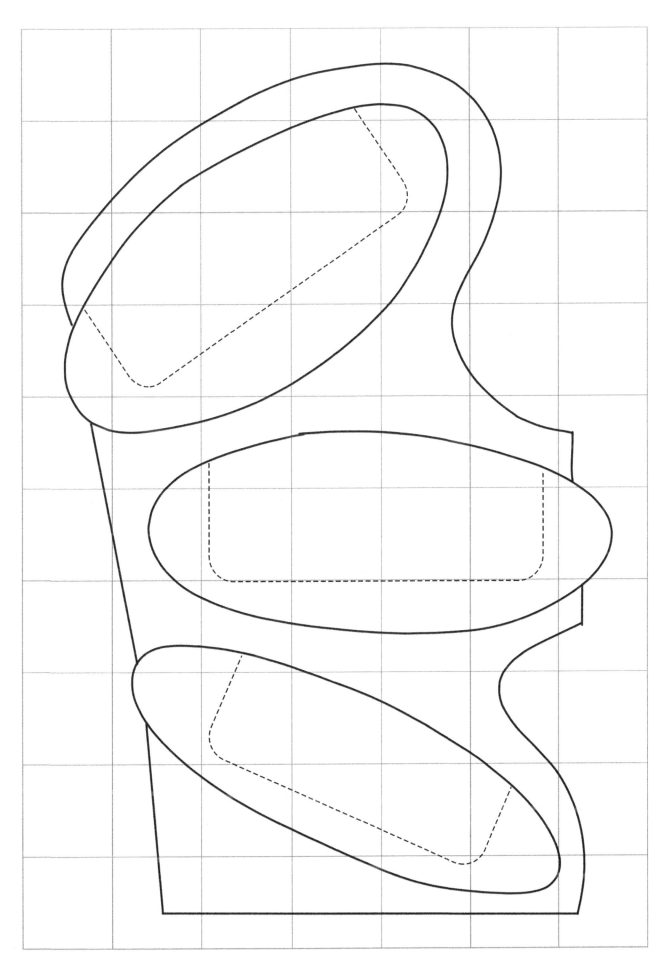

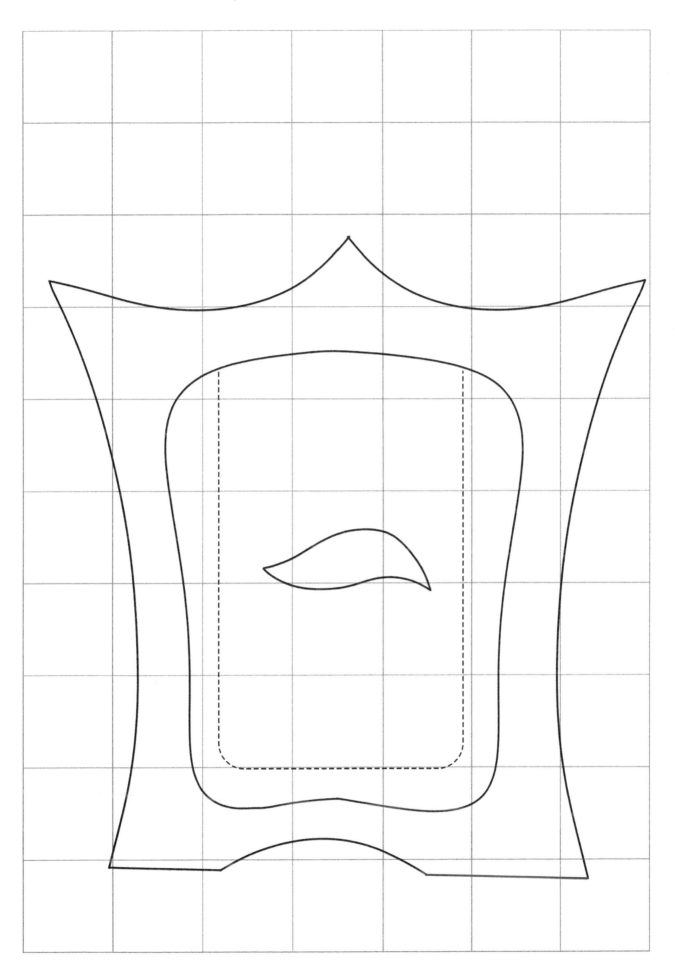

26

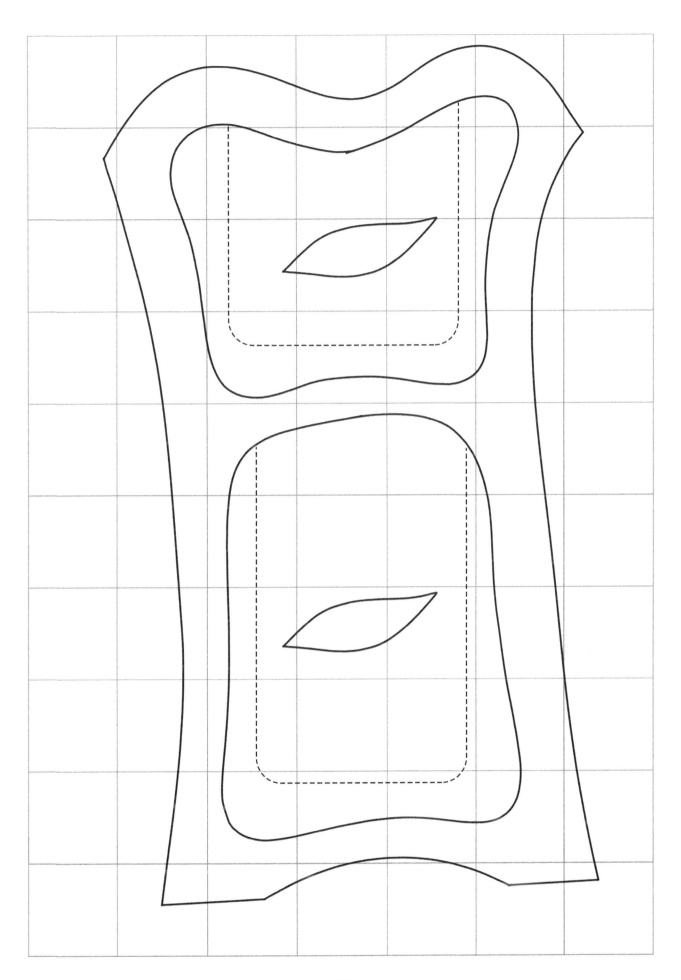

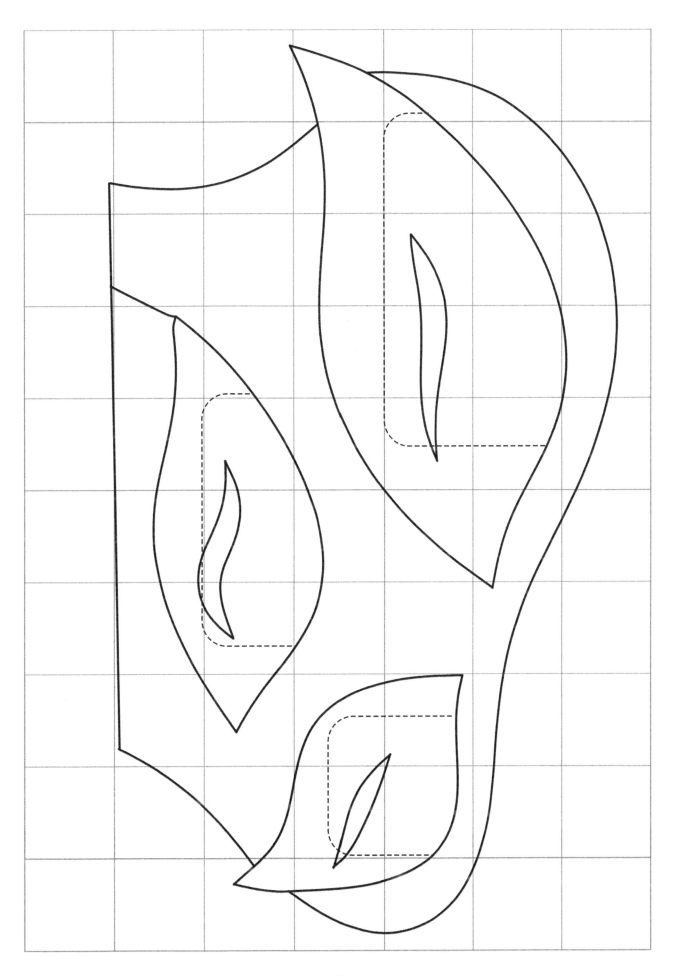

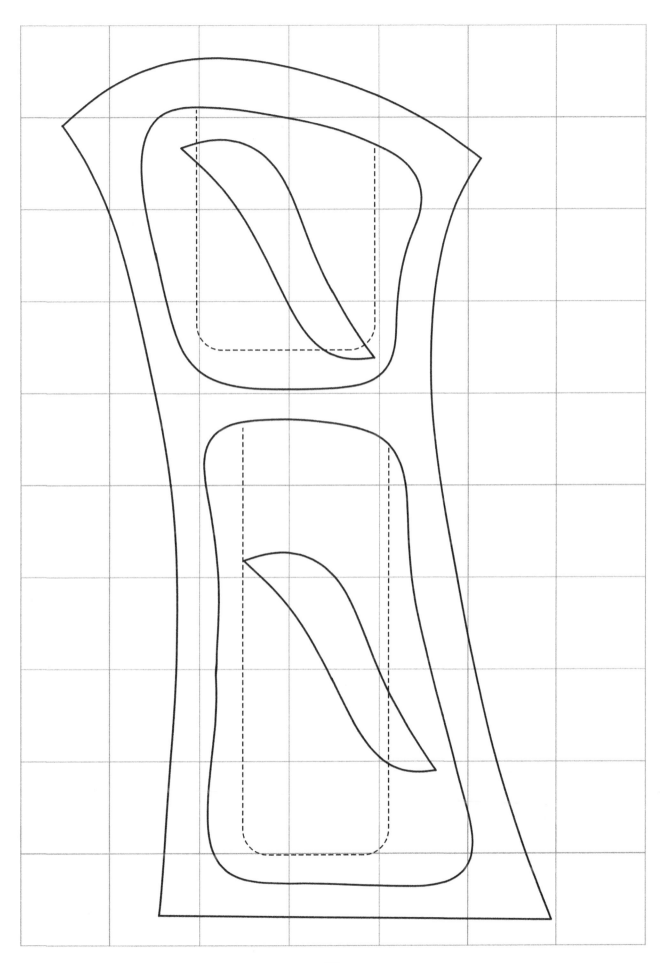

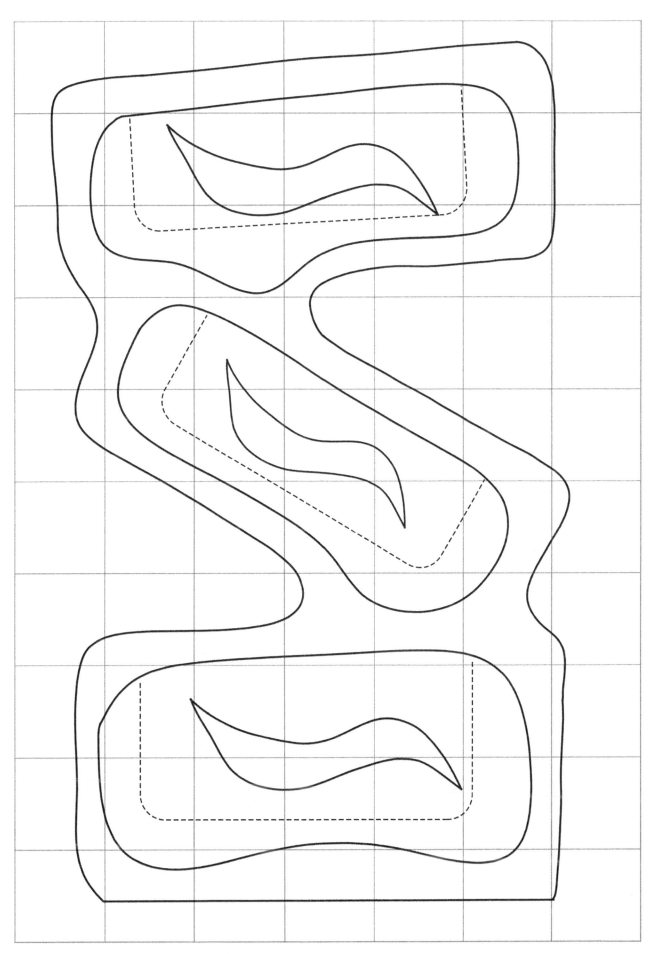

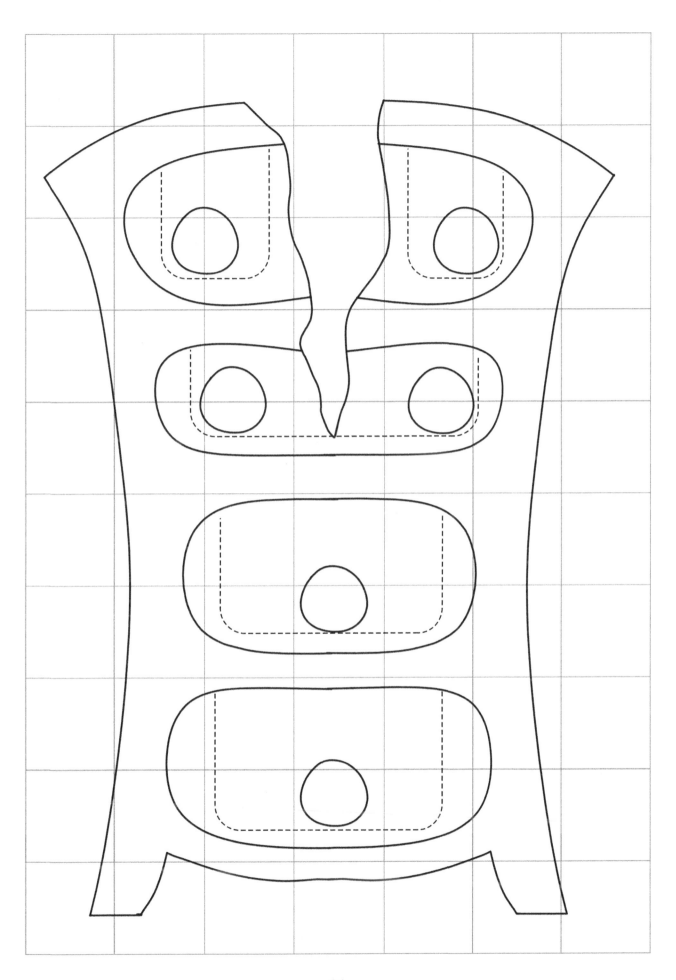

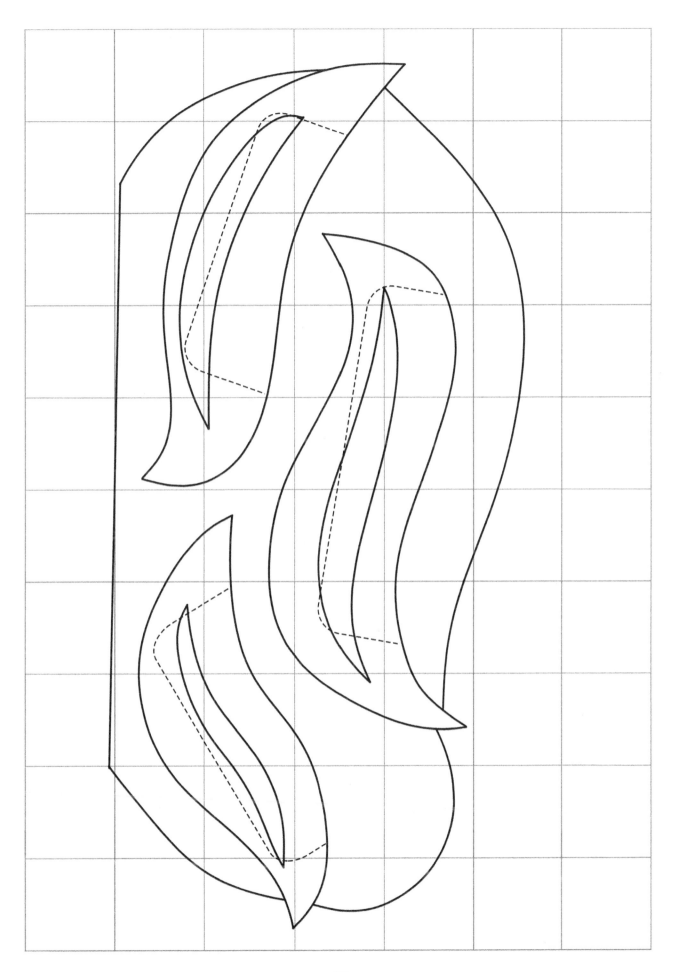

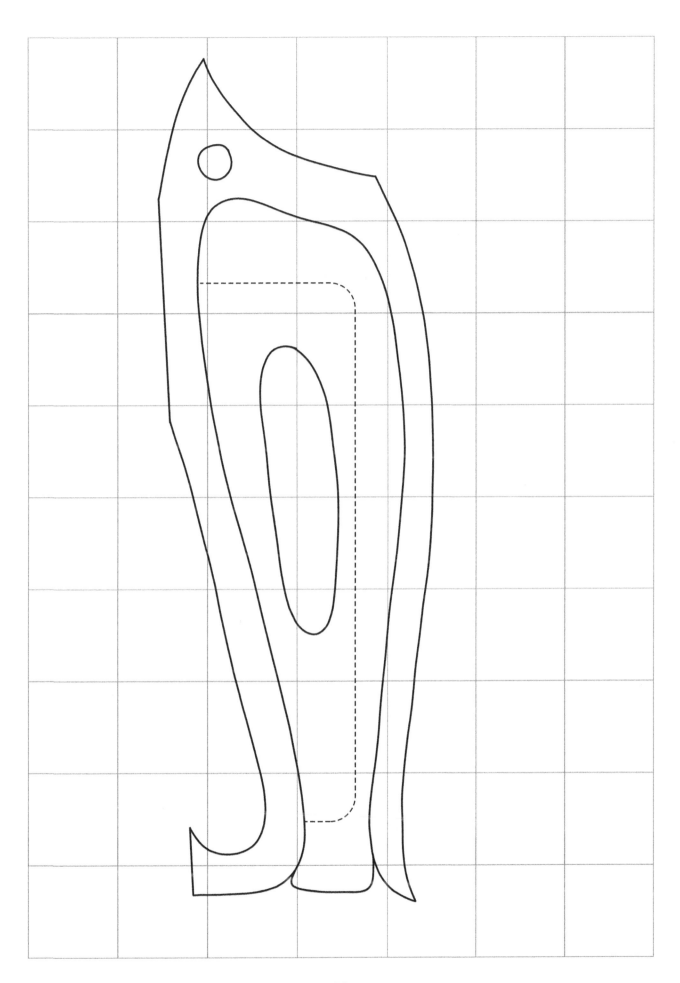

33

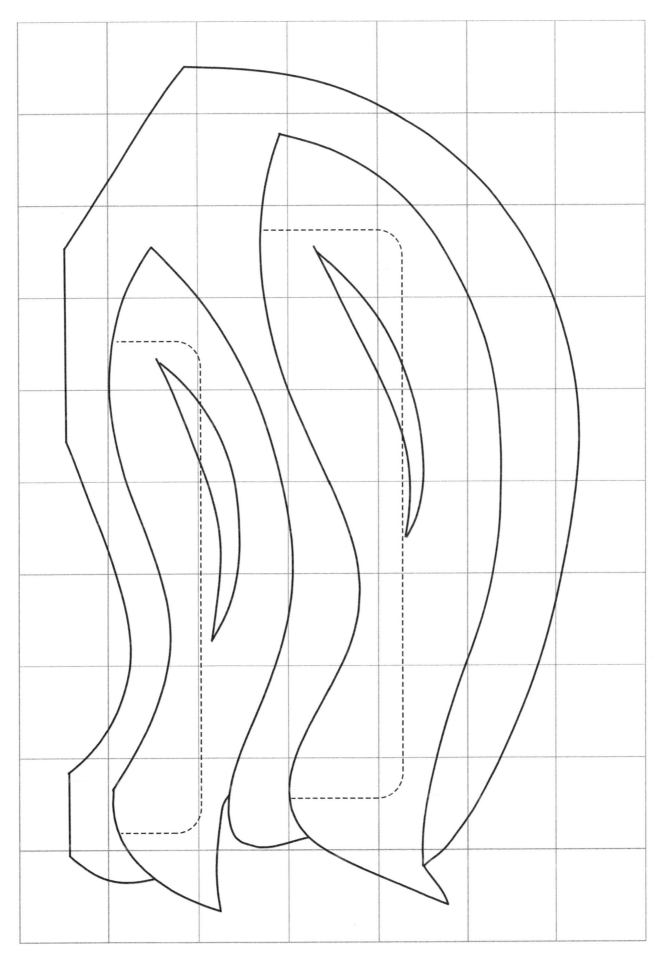

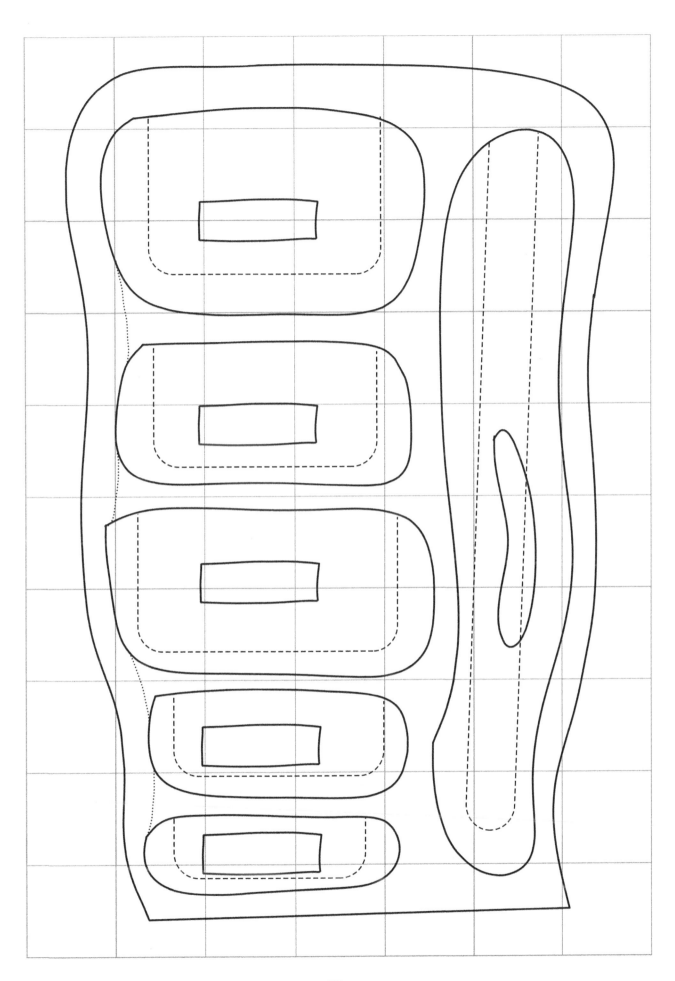

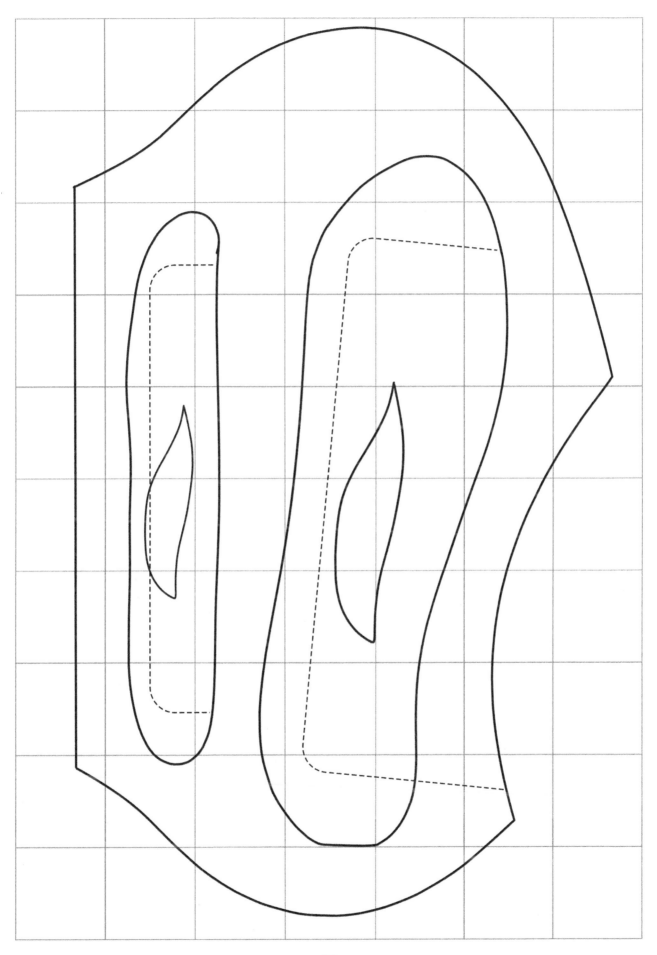

36

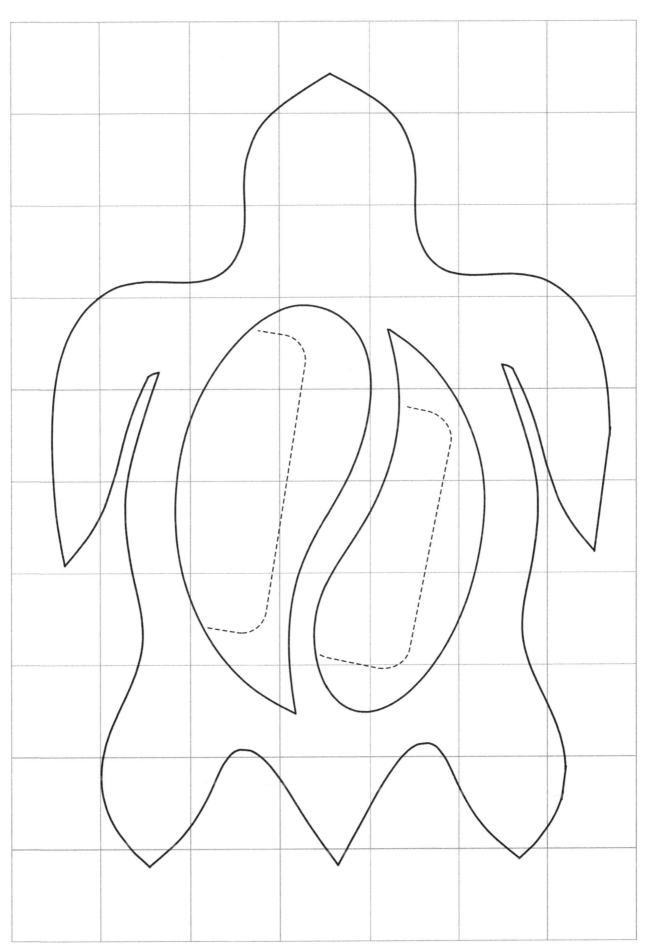

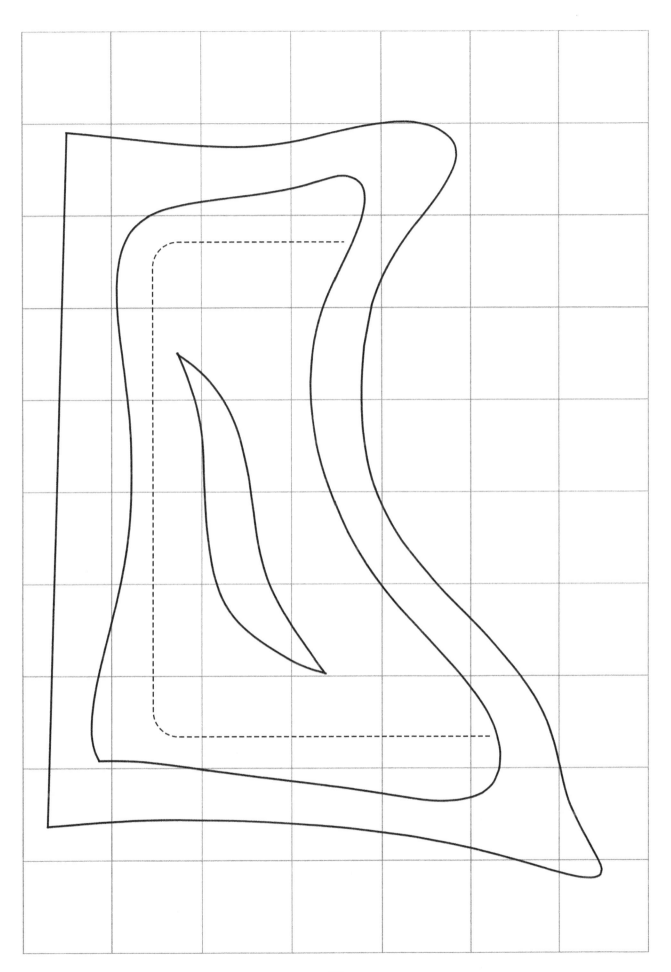

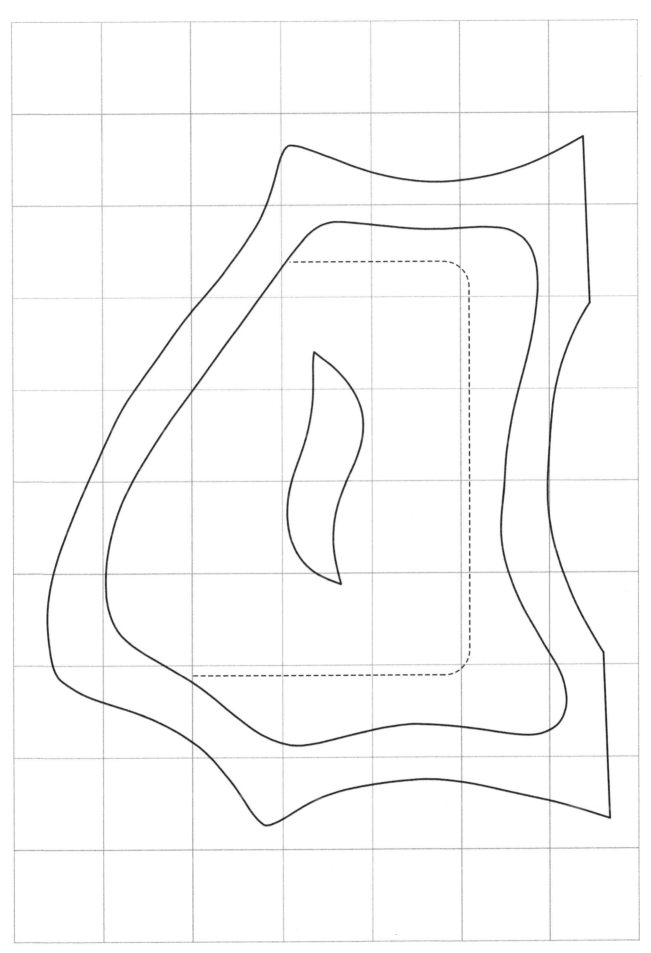

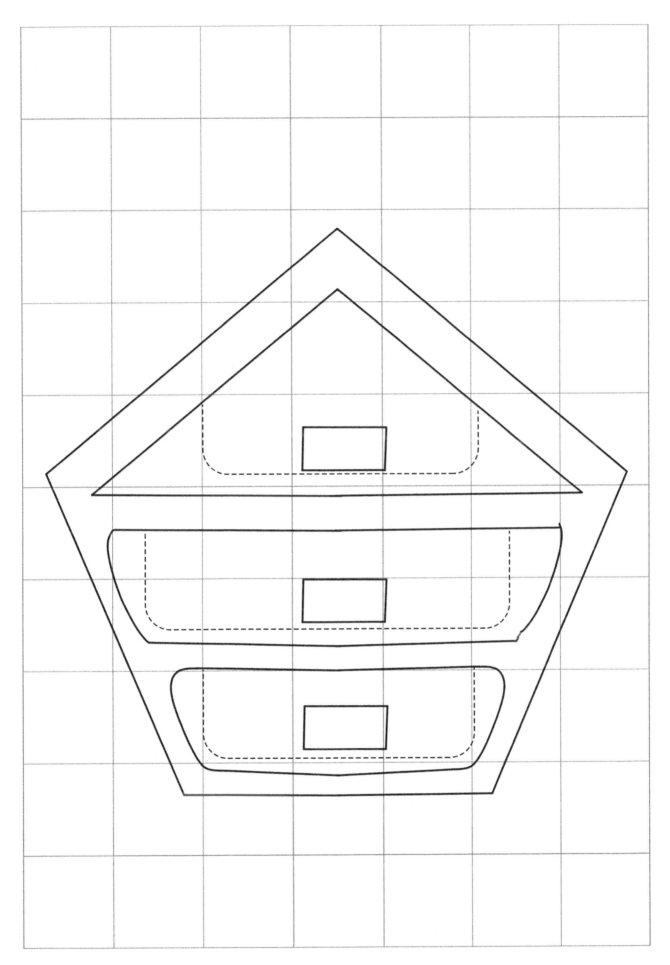

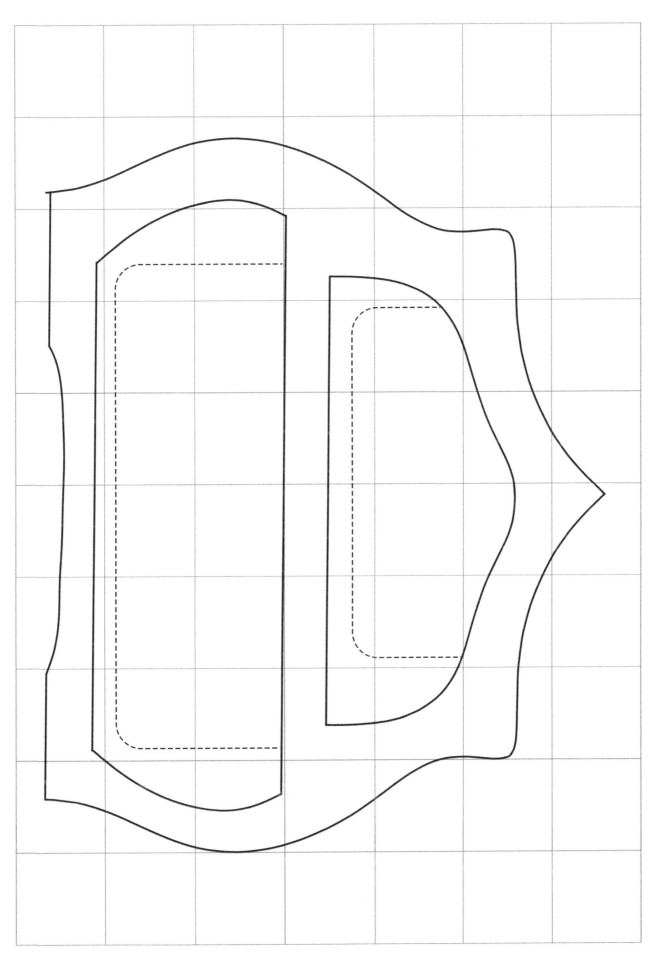

41

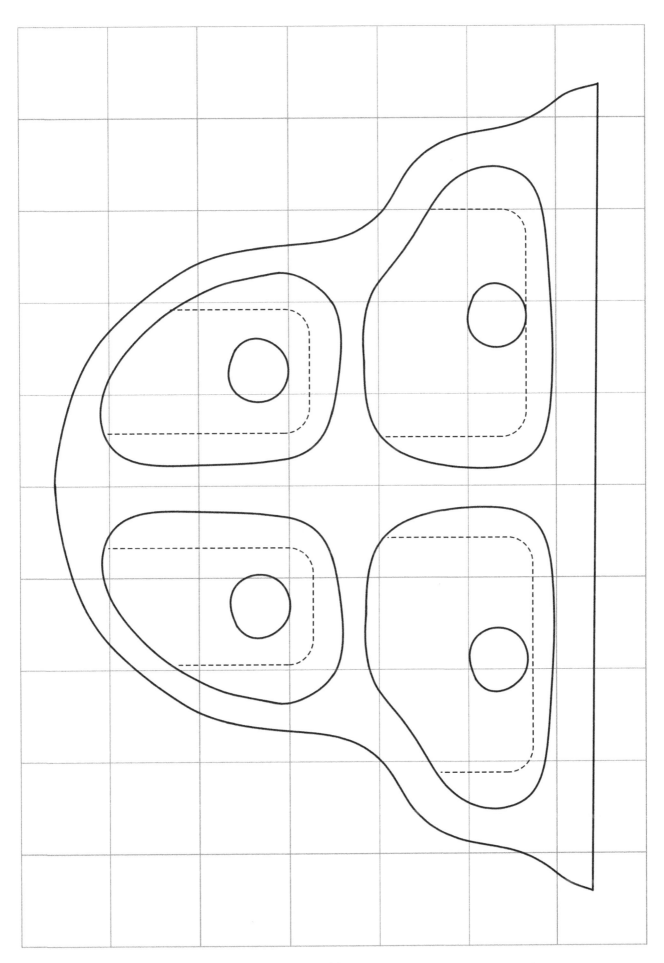

43

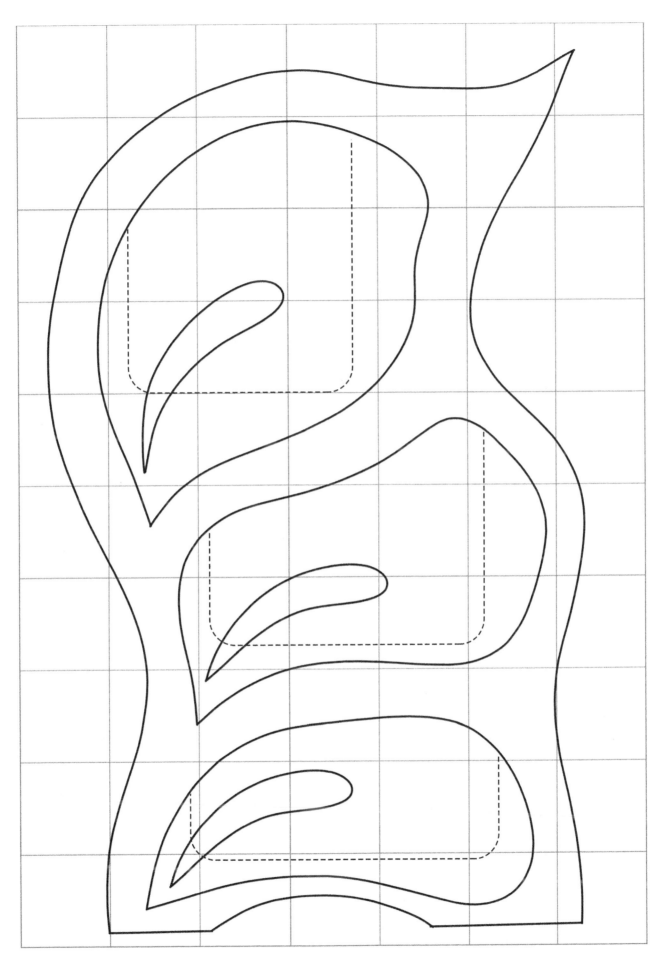

44

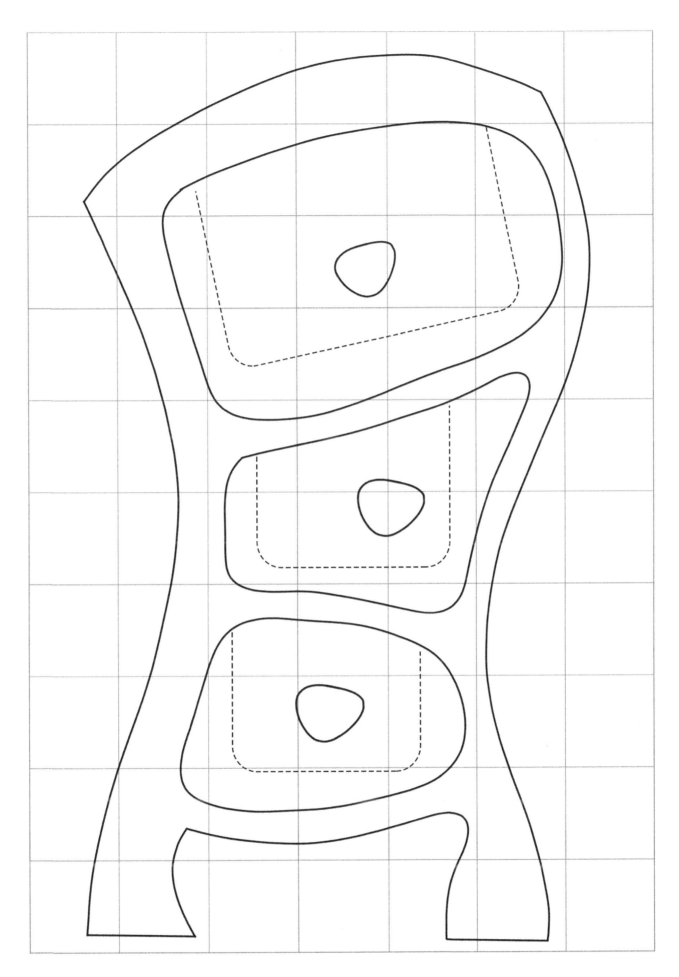

45

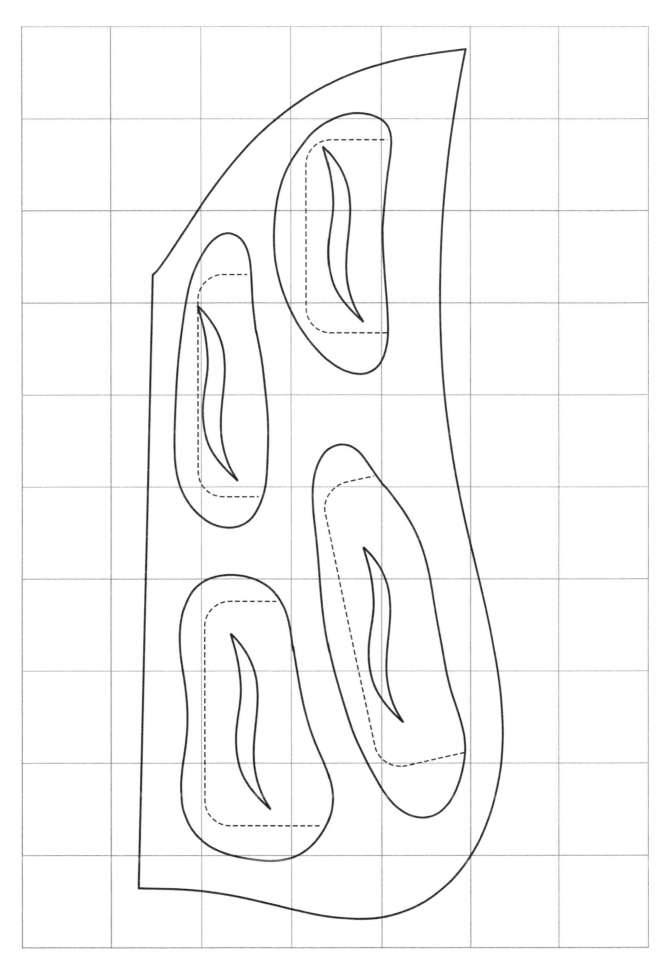

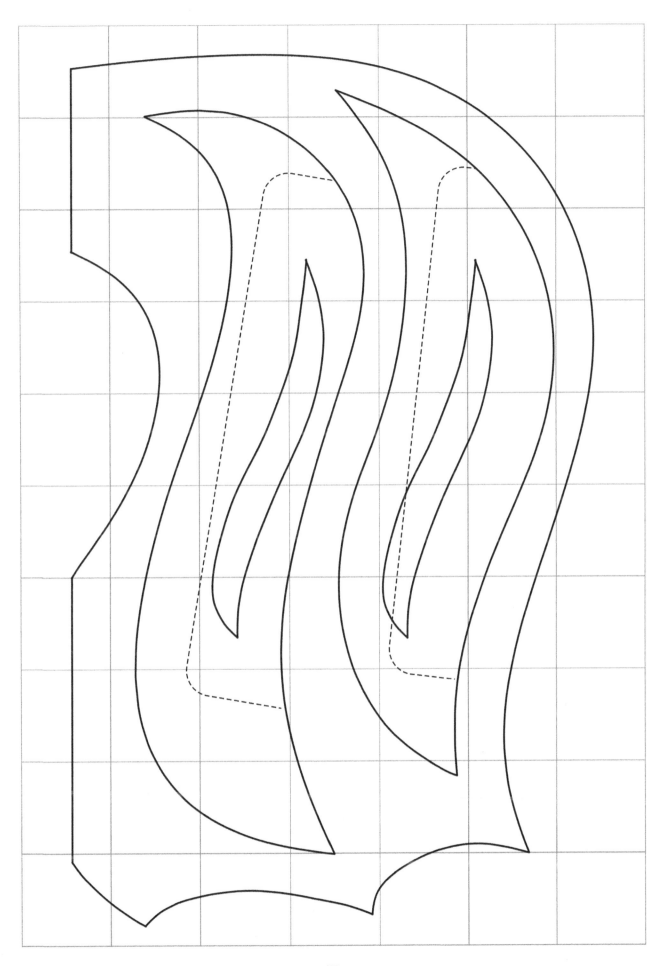

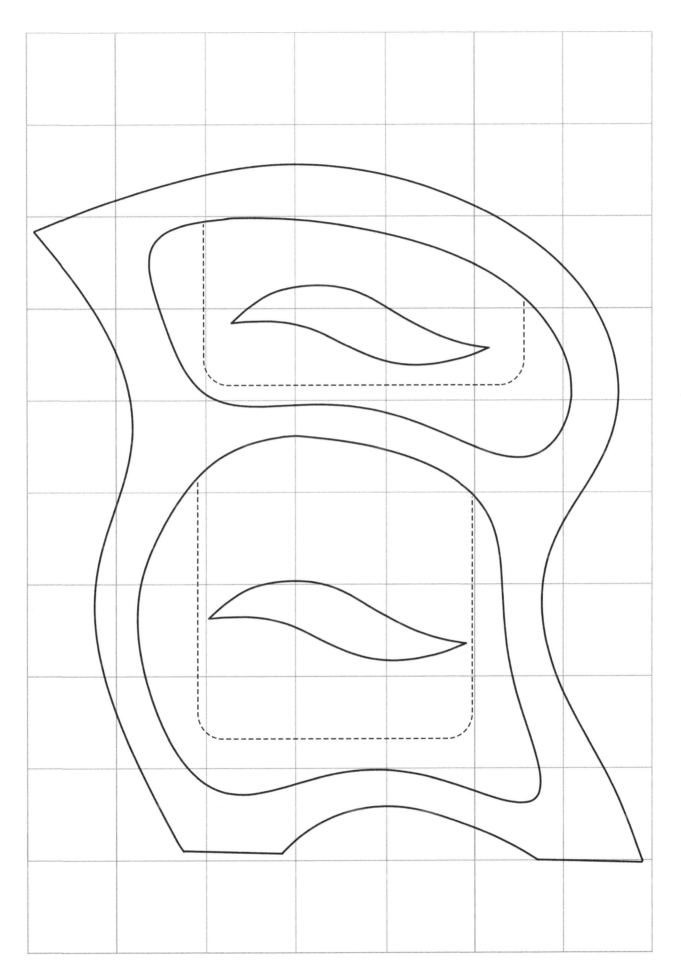

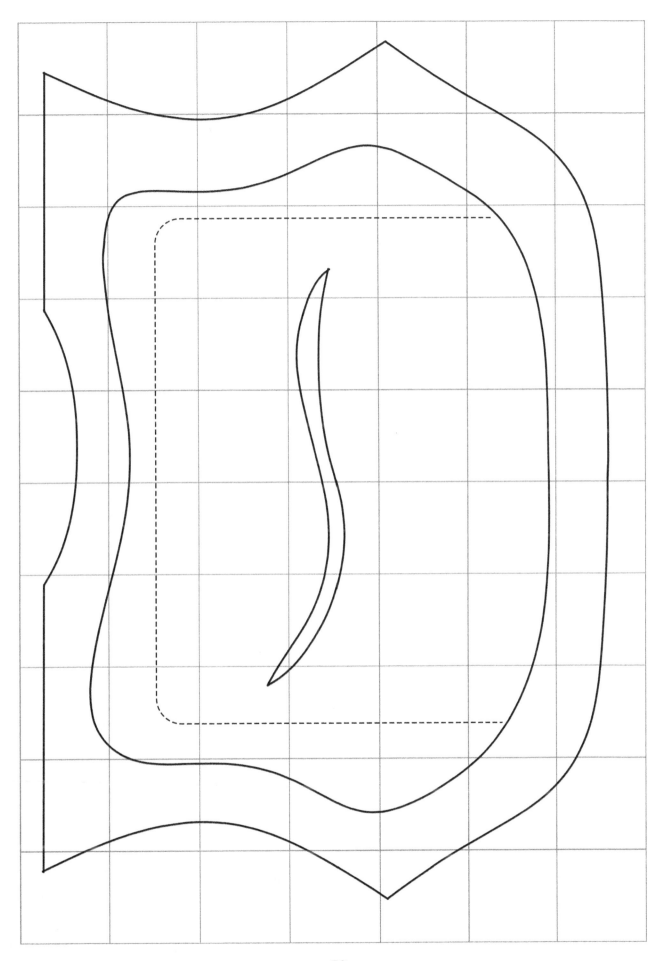

50